THE RAGBAG OF MY MIND

THE RAGBAG OF MY MIND

Bob Blane

EMERITUS PUBLISHING

First published in 2014 by Emeritus Publishing,
12 Robsland Avenue, Ayr, KA7 2RW

© Bob Blane, 2014

All rights reserved. No part of this publication may be reproduced, stored in a retrieval system, or transmitted, in any form or by any means, electronic, mechanical, photocopying, recording or otherwise, without the prior permission of the publishers and copyright holders.

Bob Blane has asserted his rights under the Copyright, Designs, and Patents Act 1988 to be identified as the author of this work.

Cover illustration: 1946 drawing of the author in the uniform of the Royal Engineers. The drawing is the work of an artist in Göttingen, Germany.

Back-cover photograph by Duncan. I. McEwan

Typeset by 3btype.com

Graphics by Mark Blackadder

Printed by Bell & Bain Ltd

ISBN: 978-1905769-43-8

To Gerry: my wife of sixty-four years

CONTENTS

1	Paddy Gunn	9
2	Bill, Albert and Bert	11
3	Faith	13
4	Roger le Grenouille	17
5	The Power of Money	19
6	Tony Collins and the Gay Future Coup	21
7	Peggy Kennedy	29
8	Pablo and the Beautiful Game	33
9	Eddie McGhee	37
10	John Rankine	39
11	Yeomanry Humour	45
12	Four Years Before the Mast	49
13	Hogmanay Incident	59
14	Bill Aitken	63
15	Getting a Start	67
16	Going the Distance	69
17	Andy, Jimmy, Dave, John and Dame Margot	71
18	À la Recherche du Conte Perdu	75
19	Angela's Ghost	77
20	Willie Carrocher	83

1

PADDY GUNN

'Look up Paddy Gunn,' said Dad.

I did so and read the entry to him.

'That's wrong,' he said. 'It was the previous day.'

Burned into Father's memory was the moment when the German sniper took Paddy out.

I never quizzed Dad further on his experience in the trenches or who Paddy was. I left all that to my imagination.

In the National War Memorial in Edinburgh Castle Dad opened out a little. But usually he was uncommunicative about his First World War days, though I recall him once saying how they used to take off their underwear, turn each item inside out and run a lighted candle up the seams to hear the satisfying crack of nits being killed by the scorching heat at the top of the flame.

So it was my imagination that formed the story of Paddy Gunn. I visualised him as an Irishman who had joined the British Army, taking the Queen's shilling and serving in the Boer War, coming through without a scratch.

In my mind Paddy never got the length of India. The

next place to beckon was France. And for Paddy it was sadly the last.

He might well have come through it too and gone home to Ireland to live on his army pension, but showing off to the two young lads at whose feet he dropped, carelessly exposing enough of himself to a well-concealed enemy marksman, ended all that.

2

BILL, ALBERT AND BERT

Bill Macrorie was a two-doors-away neighbour of mine for years. As a boy he became an apprentice butcher, handling large sides of slaughtered animals, and this led to him being picked, during his conscripted Army days, to help Albert Pierrepoint hang more than twenty convicted Japanese prisoners in Changi Jail, Singapore, after the Second World War.

Bill told me Albert was the most meticulous worker. He got every condemned man's exact weight and filled a sack with this amount. It hung overnight by the rope to be used next day. Bill explained how Albert despatched the condemned men in threes, marking with chalk a cross on the trapdoor for each to stand, and positioning men behind to ensure no one moved before the trap opened. Despite this attention to detail Bill managed to get his uniform spattered with blood once. Chinese coolies later wheeled away the corpses in a handcart to dump them in a pit.

Albert never met Ayr's town clerk, Robert C. Brown, but they corresponded. An RAF airman stationed in

Ayrshire was tried at the High Court in Ayr for the murder of an Irvine Valley girl who had been working as a house maid in a mansion in Symington, between Ayr and Kilmarnock. The jury found the man, named Withers, guilty and he was condemned to death.

To his absolute horror Bert Brown found that, as town clerk of the burgh in which the High Court had sat, it was his duty to arrange the execution of the condemned man. To Bert's intense relief – and that of Withers – the Secretary of State for Scotland commuted the sentence to one of life imprisonment. Bert held on to his correspondence with Albert and produced it on one occasion at the Water Trip, delighting his audience.

The Water Trip was a jolly which Scottish local authorities held in those days to repay council members for their otherwise unpaid work on behalf of ratepayers. Ayr's Water Trip outing was staged at Loch Recawr, which provided the town of Ayr, some thirty miles away, with the bulk of its water supply. A specially built pavilion beside the loch, housed the once-a-year visit entertaining council members and other selected guests.

After lunch and a drink or two Bert amused the guests by reading his correspondence with Albert, ending with Albert's expressed readiness to be of assistance to Bert on any future occasion, should the need arise.

3

FAITH

Sri Lanka was called Ceylon in those days. There was a war on and Willie Kerr found himself in Colombo helping defend the island against possible attack and invasion by the Japanese.

Willie was really a naval man, loving the sea and boats, but he was given a squad of foot soldiers, all local men, and left to do what he wanted. So Willie took them on a route march. He had no maps or charts. He had his uniform and footwear, but the men had no boots. They were all used to going barefoot.

The uncharted land where they found themselves had seen little of human visit for years, and when Willie decided to call a halt and bed down for the night he heard one of his men give out an agonising cry. Willie found the man had been bitten by a snake he had trodden on. Willie took out his hand gun and shot the snake dead. He knew it was a Russell's viper and the man would die in fifteen minutes.

The sudden appearance on the scene of a Buddhist monk Willie had not seen before surprised Willie. The man spoke English, telling Willie he would help the bitten man. The monk sat down and began sucking out blood from the wound and spitting it out. Willie left the two men alone as he checked to ensure his camping ground was safe to bed down on.

When Willie returned to the two men he found the bitten member of his squad sitting up talking to his help.

For the man and Willie's platoon the monk had been heaven sent. Willie's view was more pragmatic. He felt the monk had been following him for miles, hoping to be fed.

'He will be all right,' the monk told Willie. 'He has faith.' The man went to sleep as Willie and his new companion talked. They talked well into the dark.

'With faith we can move great hills,' the monk told Willie. 'Tomorrow I shall show you.'

By dawn the monk and Willie's squad were up and Willie found the bitten man proudly showing off his foot to the others. It was, for Willie, an impressive display.

The monk joined the others to eat. He told Willie: 'I had promised to show you faith.'

He joined Willie and his squad till they reached a river. Willie saw signs of crocodile presence and wondered what the monk had in mind.

'I have faith,' the man said, 'and the crocodiles will not touch me.'

He began stripping off his clothes, preparing to enter the river. Willie told the man to stop, explaining how the river was a danger to all.

The monk persisted.

As the squad looked on the monk stepped into the water and began to wade and swim across. Half way over he let out a yell and disappeared.

Willie took out his gun and fired several shots into the water. He never saw the monk again.

4

ROGER LE GRENOUILLE

I can't recall the year, but it was 31 July. From midnight it would be August and Roger could turn his thoughts to the Côte d'Azur and a holiday month of Mediterranean bliss. He had worked hard and earned it.

Roger was short, fat and instantly likeable. He beamed through the sweat streaming down his bald head as he brought each of us a plate of frogs' legs to the bare, well-scrubbed, wooden tables of his estaminet in the Latin Quarter.

We were a much-relaxed gathering of differing nationals whose differences could easily be set aside as we half-submerged in a sea of self-indulgence. Sharing my table were two Spanish women who came to Paris each summer to sell hats. Of the two Carmen had the better tale to tell. It was the story of Manolete. He was for seasons the greatest bullfighter in Spain and, therefore, the world, till Dominguin came along to challenge his supremacy.

But back in his dominant day, when General Franco organised a new lunatic asylum for Madrid, Manolete was clearly the best person to carry out the opening ceremony. That was arranged.

The next hurdle to leap was choosing someone to show Manolete round after the ceremony. A lottery was fixed for that. The boy who won hero-worshipped Manolete. The lad wanted nothing in life but to follow in the footsteps of his hero. Man and boy met and Manolete was shown the patients in the building:

'This first man,' the lad explained, 'thinks he is Napoleon Bonaparte.'

Manolete was already tired of the whole business. He wanted out to matters more pressing. He became dismissive of the lot: *'Folie de grandeur,'* he said, with a wave of his arm. 'Delusions of grandeur obviously.'

The boy was taken aback, his hero-worship seriously punctured. He said nothing, but moved on.

'This second patient thinks he is the Caudillo, General Franco.'

Manolete was even more dismissive, brushing everything aside: 'Nothing but *folie de grandeur* – delusions of grandeur.'

The lad was now totally disillusioned by his former hero and determined to get his own back. He led the way to the third patient: 'This is the most remarkable person we have,' said the lad. 'He thinks he is you – Manolete, the greatest bullfighter in the world.'

'Perfectly understandable,' said Manolete. 'Delusions of grandeur. Why is he different?'

'We've had to change his nurse five times,' said the lad. 'He keeps on slicing off her ears.'

5

THE POWER OF MONEY

George Bernard Shaw stopped Sir Henry Irving's widow when she wanted to prevent Irving being given a Westminster Abbey funeral. The Irvings had ceased living together in 1872 and got a deed of separation in 1879. When Irving died in October 1905 he had been living for years with another woman, Mrs Aria.

Irving had the most powerful dramatic ability, which he put to great use on stage. On his death General William Booth, founder of the Salvation Army, and Dr John Clifford, the Baptist leader, sought an Abbey funeral for him. Lady Irving was outraged by the idea. She wrote to Shaw, asking him to go and see her. He did. She was determined that her disgusting beast of a husband should not have such an honour thrust upon him.

Shaw was terrified. He wanted an Abbey funeral, not for Irving's sake, but for the profession's. He knew that the widow had only to send a postcard to Booth or Clifford to have the whole thing dropped.

Shaw went home and wrote Lady Irving a long letter full of sympathy, telling her that when Irving caught a cold in Manchester and wanted to go to the seaside the hat had to be sent round. This was always happening in the profession, he said, and might happen at any time to her two sons, Harry and Laurence, who had followed their father in a theatrical career.

In his letter Shaw told Lady Irving that as the widow of a great actor buried in Westminster Abbey she had only to lift her little finger and she would get a civil pension, but as the widow of a worthless scoundrel she would get nothing. That did the trick. She withdrew her opposition and shortly after got her pension. And Irving, following his cremation, got his ashes buried in the Abbey. Shaw turned down an invitation to attend.

6

TONY COLLINS AND THE GAY FUTURE COUP

Before the Gay Future fraud case called at Preston Crown Court in February 1976, Tony Collins, one of the two accused, attended an unrelated dinner.

'Where you are going,' an unfriendly fellow guest at the function told him, 'the food won't be so good.'

'Perhaps not,' said Tony, 'but the company will be better.'

Tony and co-conspirator Tony Murphy, from Douglas, Cork, in Eire, did not go to jail. They were each fined, reluctantly, £1,000 and ordered to pay £500 towards prosecution costs by Mr Justice Caulfield who disagreed with the jury's 10–2 majority decision in favour of a guilty verdict.

The trial lasted seven days and the jury were out for six hours and seventeen minutes discussing the issue. Their decision surprised more than Justice Caulfield. But it was what the Jockey Club wanted to hear and they warned both men off for ten years.

This hit Tony Collins harder than any fine. Racing had been a major part of his life for as long as he could recall.

Cork builder William Anthony Murphy was the real brain behind the Gay Future affair. Apart from Tony Collins he enlisted five friends from Ireland in his syndicate – four from Cork and one from Waterford. When the prosecution tried to extradite them from Eire they failed to do so. Only Tony Murphy stood his ground and was commended by Mr Justice Caulfield for doing so:

'You have remained a sportsman to the end,' he said, 'and there are many who would admire you for coming over to this country, acknowledging the jurisdiction of the court, and facing the jury.'

Mr Ivor Taylor QC, who had prosecuted, told the bench after the return of the verdict:

'There are a number of other men for whom the police have warrants.' He successfully applied for a warrant for the arrest of Iain McCallan, a former stable lad employed by Tony Collins, who had fled to Eire to avoid becoming a prosecution witness. I don't think that warrant and the others were implemented.

Ever since bank holidays were created by Parliament's Act of 1871, they have been popular for staging a racing coup. August, with a score of fixtures, became legendary. A trainer could enter a runner for several meetings, get it shown in the morning papers as running at one fixture then take it to another. It was widely recognised that the best place to hide a leaf was in a forest where everyone could see it, but only the initiated could point it out.

The Ulverston Novices Hurdle at Cartmel was the

race chosen for Gay Future. Two other horses of the Tony Collins string at his home, Torley, in Fullarton Woods outside Troon, became part of the plot. They were Ankerwyke, entered to run at Plumpton, and Opera Cloak, listed to appear at Southwell.

Tony Collins's wife of those days went to Cartmel to be seen, but Tony kept out of the way. So too did Ankerwyke and Opera Cloak. Neither left the yard at Torley.

When Gay Future had won by fifteen lengths at Cartmel and been returned at odds of 10/1, alarm bells started ringing. Tony Murphy had engaged a team of men to go round placing small bets in betting shops, chiefly in London, linking Gay Future with the other two horses. Doubles with the non-runners became singles on Gay Future and the syndicate stood to collect something between quarter of a million and three hundred thousand pounds.

An investigation started at once. The claim that broken-down transport had stopped Ankerwyke and Opera Cloak reaching their planned racecourses was dismissed by a phone call to Torley. It was answered by one of the domestic staff not privy to the coup:

'Oh, no,' she said. 'The horses are here. I can see them from the window.'

It is at this point that George Wigg enters the story. Having saved the nation from the dire consequences of Russian espionage, while at the same time destroying John Profumo's chances of becoming prime minister, George had turned his attention to the pressing matter of cleaning up his beloved sport of horse racing.

George was widely regarded as the House of Commons bookie. After joining the Racecourse Betting Control Board in 1957 and the Horserace Totalisator Board in 1961, he became chairman of the Horserace Betting Levy Board, succeeding Lord Harding, who had narrowly escaped being assassinated while serving as Governor General of Cyprus, where Archbishop Makarios and Georgeios Grivas were trying to rid the island of British rule.

George Wigg did more than anyone else to break the Jockey Club's stranglehold on racing and banish their eighteenth-century thinking from the sport. Always a master of intrigue – it was called wiggery pokery in the House of Commons – George helped Harold Wilson beat George Brown to the Labour Party leadership after Hugh Gaitskell died. George was rewarded with the paymaster-general's job when Harold Wilson took over in Downing Street.

But George soon became a thorn in Harold Wilson's side and Harold eventually got rid of him by making him chairman of the Levy Board and a life peer as Baron Wigg, moving him to the House of Lords. This gave George control over the levy coming in from the Tote and bookmakers. George wanted this money spent his way and not the Jockey Club's. It was a duel George's side won.

The Gay Future coup was too much for George. He instructed Detective Chief Inspector Terry O'Connell of the Serious Fraud Squad to go up to Troon and nail Tony Collins. Accompanied by a detective inspector, Terry arrived in Troon and booked in to the now-defunct Sun Court Hotel overlooking Royal Troon Championship Golf Course. He contacted Bert Russell, CID sergeant at Ayr, inviting him to the Sun Court to share its splendid hospitality and cuisine.

Each night Terry phoned George to update him on progress – or the lack of it. The investigation was hampered by the fact that one of Tony Collins' stable lads had Hodgkin's disease and was being treated in hospital in Glasgow.

But Terry realised he had hit a brick wall when Bert Russell told him no crime or offence had been committed in Scots law. And that is why the case went to Preston Crown Court. The two men were charged with conspiring to defraud by betting on three horses when they knew only one would run. It seemed to many a flimsy indictment. A majority of the jury did not think so, and their decision barred the two men from their sport.

A television film of the Gay Future coup, entitled *Murphy's Stroke*, was made with Pierce Brosnan in the cast in those days before he became 007 James Bond. It was 22 July 1986, when Tony Collins was allowed to return to the sport which had absorbed his interest in the past. He got back into winning vein with Chance Remark, a horse he owned in partnership with two others. It won the Lothians Novice Hurdle at Musselburgh on 8 January 1988, trained by Jonjo O'Neill.

From boyhood and Harrow days Tony Collins saw the law as a tiresome restriction that did not apply to him. The Collins family had made a fortune printing the Holy

Bible in Glasgow. Tony worked for a time with the thread firm of Coats in Paisley. He ran around in a red MG sports car TZ 4747. The police arrested him for driving whilst unfit through drink or drugs. He appeared in court from overnight custody, pleaded not guilty to the charge, explained to the court he was about to marry, had a trial date fixed then disappeared to Spain.

Home for Tony in those days was Milton Dower House, where his widowed mother lived, on the South Ayrshire estate of Blairquhan, owned by Sir James Hunter Blair. When Tony returned there from Spain the village constable spotted him. Not wanting to be too closely involved in taking action against Tony, the constable phoned his headquarters in Ayr and two officers went out to pick him up for disposal of the long-pending case.

Tony did his National Service alongside the late Robert Sangster, heir to the Vernons football-pools fortune. The two men became great friends and Sangster named more than one of his horses after Tony. As a point-to-point rider Tony Collins was absolutely fearless. When Bogside racecourse was closed down to racing after the 1965 Scottish Grand National meeting, it was bought by ICI to sterilise development and protect the neighbouring explosives works at Ardeer. But point-to-point meetings were allowed and the course was used by Eglinton Hunt and also the Lanark and Renfrew Hunt. Tony was instrumental in getting Ayrshire Yeomanry to stage point-to-point racing there as well. I recall seeing him take a crashing fall at a tricky fence in the back straight. He was stretchered into an ambulance and wheeled off to Kilmarnock Infirmary.

After he moved to Torley, Tony infuriated the members of Royal Troon Golf Club by hacking his horses across their links to access the beach and foreshore at Troon for use as gallops.

Though racing's ruling body and the police had time and again to put Tony in his place, no-one did it better than Sanny Dobbie, the pipe-smoking, gravel-voiced constable at the desk in Ayr police office. Tony had been told to report to the office over a traffic offence and eventually did so. Sanny had the job of noting down Tony's personal details. PC Dobbie chewed laconically on his pipe stem and eyed Tony up and down.

'Yes,' said Sanny in his bass voice. 'I'll need some information. First of all your name.'

'Anthony Kenneth Collins,' said Tony.

'Anthony . . . Kenneth . . . Collins,' Sanny intoned as he wrote down the name, his voice sinking ever lower to basso profundo. Sanny jotted down Tony's date of birth and home address, then realised he had failed to record Tony's profession.

'Occupation?' asked Sanny.

Tony drew himself up to his full five feet eight inches.

'Gentleman,' he announced.

'Yes,' said Sanny. 'Yes.' His voice sank to its lowest possible, audible pitch. He bit on his pipe stem, removed the pipe from his mouth, eyed Tony up and down once more then asked his final question:

'Would that no' be apprentice chentleman?'

7

PEGGY KENNEDY

As an 18-year-old youth in 1777 Robert Burns went to the South Ayrshire village of Kirkoswald to study mensuration, surveying, dialling – hoping to qualify for a well-paid job as an exciseman. It was here, he said, that he learnt to fill his glass and mix without fear in a drunken squabble.

Kirkoswald seemed an unlikely place to study mensuration, but there were excise officials there keeping an eye on the Kennedys at Culzean Castle, two miles away for a crow in flight.

The Kennedys were the hub in the wheel which brought to the mainland market the whisky illegally distilled on Arran and the Isle of Man. They gave up this trade when they found their sailing ship, *Lord Cassillis*, could be employed more profitably carrying fit, young Africans from the west coast of Africa across the Atlantic to fill the demand for labour on the plantations of the West Indies and the south-east of North America.

Robert Burns was himself nearly involved in this business, intending to go to the Indies with Highland Mary Campbell, but was persuaded against that move by the success in the summer of 1786 of the *Kilmarnock Edition* of his poems, and he went instead to Edinburgh to arrange a second edition. Here he met members of the city's high society.

Peggy Kennedy was not directly a Culzean Kennedy, but she was related. Her father had the South Ayrshire estate of Daljarrock, on the right bank of the river Stinchar, a dozen miles upstream from its mouth at Ballantrae. Peggy had an aunt, Mrs Gavin Hamilton, whose husband was a good friend of Burns. As a girl of 17 Peggy was introduced to Burns who was later to write his best-known love song, which achieved worldwide acclaim, about her.

In the summer of 1785 Peggy was betrothed to Captain Maxwell, of the Galloway family, which would later produce *Ring of Bright Water* author Gavin Maxwell. Peggy, however, fell for the charms of Captain McDouall, of Logan, who was 25 and the MP for Wigtownshire.

Burns learned her story and wrote a song, putting into Peggy's mouth the words:

Ye banks and braes o' bonie Doon,
How can ye bloom sae fresh and fair!
How can ye chant, ye little birds,
And I sae weary fu' o' care!

Thou'll break my heart, thou warbling bird,
That wantons thro' the flowering thorn;
Thou minds me o' departed joys,
Departed never to return.

Oft hae I rov'd by bonie Doon,
To see the rose and woodbine twine;
And ilka bird sang o' its luve,
And fondly sae did I o' mine.

Wi' lightsome heart I pu'd a rose,
Fu' sweet upon its thorny tree;
And my fause luver staw my rose,
But, ah! he left the thorn wi' me.

The thorn turned out to be a girl, and lawyers for Peggy raised an action against the father seeking declarator of marriage and legitimacy, with an alternative claim of damages in case of failure. Peggy died, in her twenties, after the legal process started, but it was continued on the daughter's behalf.

Peggy's legal team got judgment in favour of the marriage, but the Court of Session, on review, reversed this judgment and ordered instead a payment of £3,000 to the daughter. She went on to marry and live in nineteenth century Edinburgh.

8

PABLO AND THE BEAUTIFUL GAME

Pablo Picasso was clearly annoyed with me when I took a photograph of him without permission. It was summer. It was morning. It was Golfe Juan on the east side of Cannes. He was coming towards me on the other footpath. He was small, bald, bronzed and wearing shorts and sandals. Beside him, clutching his left forearm, was a young, blonde-haired woman. I realised afterwards she was Francoise Gilot. They had met in Paris in 1943. She had gone with him when he left the city to move to Vallauris.

Golfe Juan is the place where Napoleon landed after his escape from Elba. He went on to Paris, raised an army, and met at Waterloo a defeat which changed the face and history of much of Europe. None of this mattered to Pablo. His immediate concern was me. I had snatched a photograph with my Voigtlander Bessa 46 and there was little he could do about it. He carried on walking with Francoise. I never saw him again; nor him me.

I have long since lost that photograph. It was not a very good one.

I was in Golfe Juan to meet my brother, Jack. He and three other Scots had signed to play football with the Cannes-Grasse Club in the 1947/48 season. They were staying in the Hotel Napoleon which was run by a member of the club's board of directors, Monsieur Bacchaloni. The three others were: Alison Hutton, a nephew of the former Scottish international player 'Big Jock' Hutton; Seton Airlie, who had been released by Glasgow Celtic; and Malky McLaren. He had been playing with the Paisley club, St Mirren, which wanted money for his transfer and did not get any.

Of the four Malky was by far the best player. He caught the attention of the fans who speedily labelled him '*comique*' when they saw his ball-juggling. He also caught the attention of officials in the Italian club Roma who wanted to sign him to play in the Italian league. For Malky there was more money there.

The beautiful game has changed out of recognition since those days. Each team started with eleven players. Any player sent off by the referee for a misdemeanour reduced that team to ten. If a player was injured and could not continue, he could not be replaced. Substitution was unheard of.

This had direct bearing on Malky's projected transfer to Roma. Clubs wanted men who could play relentlessly for ninety minutes. The Roma officials completed all the details of the proposed transfer and asked Malky for his passport to complete arrangements. Malky, without thinking, handed it over. It revealed to the Roma officials that he was 29 years of age. They instantly cancelled the planned transfer.

9

EDDIE McGHEE

The Yukon gold rush had petered out by the time Eddie McGhee was old enough to leave home in search of overnight, instant riches. At 13 years of age he was an underground worker in the Ayrshire coalfield. He returned there after four-and-a-half years in Kitchener's army, serving in the Dardanelles, Egypt, the Balkans and South Russia.

Eddie and his brothers agreed South Africa was the place to be. It had diamonds as well as gold. Places with names like Kimberley had a magic about them. The brothers booked to join a ship from Southampton which would take them there. At the port they found their transport strikebound, so they stepped on the ship next door. It took them to the United States of America.

Eddie got a job with Bell Telephone Company in Chicago. He had lodgings near a florist's shop in the city.

'It was a wonderful place,' said Eddie, 'with a waterfall and flowing water.' The owner reputedly got flowers from Mexico and South America.

Eddie returned to his lodgings from work one day to

see the shop swarming with police. He soon heard the reason. A car with three men in it had driven up. The driver stayed at the wheel. The two others walked in to the shop and shot the owner dead.

He was Dion O'Banion. His shop was the front for his racketeering activities which clashed with those of the Torrio brothers. Johnny Torrio had brought in Alphonse Capone from New York to strengthen his organisation. Al took over when Johnny found it advisable to quit the scene.

Capone became effective mayor of Chicago. He paid police and others it was convenient to bribe as he organised rackets in protection, gambling, prostitution and, principally, bootlegging which sprang from the prohibition legislation introduced after the First World War. He was not brought to account for the 250 murders he allegedly arranged across the city, the most notorious being those of Bugs Moran's gang in a garage on Valentine's Day, 1929, when his men dressed in police uniforms before carrying out the killings. City and state authorities did not curb Capone's activities, so the federal government stepped in and he was found guilty of tax evasion and sent to Alcatraz.

Eddie McGhee never got to South Africa. He worked for a time in Canada before returning to the Ayrshire coalfield. His brother Terence stayed on in America, running a successful business as a jeweller. Their father and my maternal granny, Jeanie McGhee, were cousins.

10

JOHN RANKINE

A. B. Todd sought to dispel some of the myths that grew around the name of Robert Burns, particularly opprobrious ones. Of several men he knew who had known Burns, and of those his father knew who had been acquainted with the bard, not one spoke of seeing Burns intoxicated, or angry, or of hearing him utter an oath, said Todd.

'He may, however, have been profane when he was really angry, and he had good cause to be; just as crusty old Carlyle is said to have cursed like a Castle Douglas carter at the Craigenputtoch flitting.'

Burns had a natural harmony with animals. Todd's mother recalled from the days when Burns farmed Mossgiel an occasion when the poet arrived at Auchmillan limeworks with two horses and carts. He showed a wonderful kindliness and gentleness to his horses. Though standing at a distance they would come up to him at his call and he would gently rub their eyes.

Todd enjoyed in later years, in recognition of his services to literature, a Royal Bounty List pension in those days before the Liberal Party pushed through legislation introducing old age pensions, Lloyd George forcing the House of Lords to pass the necessary Bill by threatening to swamp the Lords with Liberal peers to outvote the existing Tory majority.

Todd's father, Matthew Todd, knew Robert Burns and met him frequently at Kilmarnock market. One acquaintance of A. B. Todd, Hugh Merry, recalled his grandfather saying Burns was the kindest-hearted and best-natured man he had ever known. The grandfather was John Rankine, who farmed at Adamhill, near Tarbolton. He was a good friend of Burns.

Rankine's daughter, Annie, married John Merry, Hugh's father. Annie sat beside Burns in Mauchline kirk on the Sunday he saw a louse crawling on the bonnet of a lady in a pew in front, an incident which evoked from Burns some of his most-quoted lines.

Annie, the same age as Burns, was pursued and wooed by him. He would escort her home from social gatherings, and once filled her head so full of stories about ghosts inhabiting the clumps of trees on the dark roadside that Annie arrived home in a state of terror. Burns was so severely rebuked by the girl's mother next day, on arriving to ask after Annie, that he said afterwards: 'I never had sic a downsettin' in my life.'

Annie, in later life, lived in Cumnock with her husband, John Merry. Her souvenirs of Burns included a fine miniature portrait and a tea-caddy, both of which he had given her. She kept to her dying day some locks of Burns's hair.

When a Glasgow admirer of the poet called on her once to talk about Burns and see the relics she had of the bard, Annie parted with some of the hairs. Such a gift is designed to increase, rather than satisfy, demand, and when Annie received further requests from other Burns enthusiasts for some of the poet's hair, she answered them by sending some locks of her own without divulging the source.

'I'll just gi'e them a bit o' my ain,' said Annie. 'It's the same colour.'

Annie was one of several women who claimed in later life to have been responsible for making Burns so happy that night among the 'Corn Rigs'. Her claim was as good as, if not better than, the rest. When Annie met Burns after the song was published she told him she had not expected to be celebrated by him in print.

'Oh, aye,' said Robin, 'I was just wanting to put you in wi' the lave.'

Annie Rankine's father, John, played host at Adamhill on one occasion to Burns and the Rev. John M'Math, assistant to Dr Peter Wodrow, parish minister of Tarbolton. M'Math was on good terms with Burns who addressed a poem to him enclosing a copy of 'Holy Willie's Prayer', which the minister wanted, after Burns moved from Lochlea farm, Tarbolton, to Mossgiel farm, Mauchline.

M'Math, who was one of the 'New Licht' tendency in the kirk, had a reputation as an excellent preacher but became hypochondriac and dissipate, resigned his charge, became a soldier and died in some obscurity on the Isle of Mull in 1825.

After the visit of M'Math and Burns to Rankine's home, word got around that the assistant minister had been intoxicated at Adamhill. Notice was sent to Rankine that the kirk session was arriving on a certain day to investigate the matter.

John Rankine, who was notorious as a wag in the district, decided to give the members of the session a meal, but it was not quite ready when they arrived. He welcomed the session warmly and offered them a glass of toddy while they waited for dinner. The meal was still not quite ready, so the session members were induced to take another glass. Then they had dinner.

Rankine had arranged that a kettle of whisky was at hand to be used liberally as hot water during the meal. When dinner was over he told his guests: 'Now, gentlemen, we will have a glass of toddy and then to business.' The session members had become very talkative by this time and no one resisted when Rankine told them: 'Well, gentlemen, one glass more and then to business.'

Since Rankine himself was making the toddy it was powerful, in line with his intention, and the glasses he handed to the kirk elders were large ones. The session forgot the business they had come to Adamhill to discuss, and everyone was so drunk that no one could walk.

It was high summer and broad daylight. Rankine got his man to yoke up a hay cart into which the kirk elders were lifted, huddled together and driven home. Each man was let off at his doorstep in Tarbolton village, reeling drunk, much to the consternation of the watching villagers.

And nothing more was heard in the kirk session of Mr M'Math's intoxicated state in the company of Burns and Rankine at Adamhill.

11

YEOMANRY HUMOUR

Sir Thomas Houldsworth was not chairman at the 1952 reunion dinner, but he gave the wittiest speech.

Chairman John Vallance, a farmer from Stranraer, told the 150 at the gathering – most of them First World War survivors – about one campaign he was in:

> While the yeomanry were tough, none was tougher than Sergeant-Major John King. After we had taken a particular objective, an issue of rum was made to the men. Sergeant-Major King and I got the idea that the only place there was likely to be any buckshee rum would be at headquarters. To get there we had to pass through the lines of the Norfolk Regiment and when we were attempting this we were stopped by an officer who, by his dress, was only a few days out from home. When this officer remonstrated with us and told us to turn back, King said: 'Hey, my boy, the Turks couldn't stop us and I'm damned sure you won't stop me.'

Sir Thomas eclipsed all others that night. He was commanding the Kilmarnock squadron when war broke out:

> I was awakened from my slumbers in the middle of the night or very early in the morning of August 8, 1914, in the George Hotel, Kilmarnock, which no longer exists. I was roused by one of the staff in the hotel who said I was wanted at once on the telephone. I went down and found it was our adjutant in Ayr, Captain Montgomery, who said in a very brief and precise message: 'Take your squadron with all speed at once to Cupar, Fife, without delay.'
>
> I started towards the railway station to see what arrangements I could make. I met a policeman on the way who asked if I had heard the latest rumour to the effect that the German fleet had sunk the British fleet in the North Sea and the Germans were going to land on the coast of Fife.
>
> I said: 'You needn't worry. It's okay. I'm going to make arrangements to take the Kilmarnock squadron to Cupar, and if they have landed we will push them back.' I think it rather comforted him.
>
> When we got to the Forth Bridge the train stopped and the rumour went round that the Germans had blown up the bridge. However, after a short interval the train moved on and we went over the bridge.
>
> As we got nearer to Fife we ran into very thick mist and an optimist in our party said this was the very best thing that could happen as he understood that the great majority of Germans wore spectacles and would not be able to see in the mist, and we, with our better vision, would be able to pop them off.

Sir Thomas recalled the regiment's two previous reunions, both of which he attended. The first of these was in Ayr town hall in 1919.

> For some reason we held a reunion in 1938 in the County Buildings. I believe Captain Turner was responsible for getting that reunion together, and if I remember right it was a very cheery affair – so cheery that the County Council decided they would never let the County Buildings again.
>
> What I remember best was the entry of the colonel's old black charger, The Plug. Captain Turner thought it would be a very good idea if the colonel's charger could be introduced into the banqueting hall. But The Plug could not be found and Captain Turner had the brilliant idea of going up to Glasgow and borrowing one of those skins used in pantomimes on the stage and he brought this down and he induced two individuals to get inside it.
>
> Colonel Boswell was in the chair and when the critical moment arrived and the colonel's charger was due to make an appearance, no sooner had The Plug entered the banqueting hall than it collapsed on the floor and we had considerable difficulty getting the two individuals out. I think they were carried away on a stretcher.

12

FOUR YEARS BEFORE THE MAST

Willie Robertson was a wild boy who ran away from home three times, wanting to join a windjammer crew and get to sea. On one occasion he was brought back by the skipper of the ship he tried to board at Glasgow's Broomielaw.

Willie was 23 before he got his wish and his first sea voyage, towing down the Thames and casting off in the Channel to set sail for Adelaide. By then he had given seven years to newspaper work and he returned to it, eventually owning his own paper which he started at the age of 32 in 1880. It remained his till his death in 1924. He had spent four of his seventy-six years before the mast.

The voyage to Australia whetted Willie's appetite for sea life. The later trip that tempered his sea fever was his journey and return round the Horn before the Panama Canal was cut. It failed to quench his thirst totally, for he spent another two years going to sea.

That first voyage, which began in 25 October 1871, was on a Clyde-built barque, the *Girvan*, with lines like a yacht. On the outward trip they never had a bad day. Crossing the equator Willie was initiated to the mysteries of Neptune and sea traditions. He was given a shave by the rest of the crew. He saw his first dolphin, hooked his first tunny and killed his first shark.

In his unpublished diaries Willie observes:

> In the Southern Ocean away down among the albatrosses and Cape pigeons, we had storm petrels as constant companions. The birds joined the ship in the English Channel and were still with her when she reached Kangaroo Island guarding the entrance to the Gulf of St Vincent. The petrels followed under the taffrail night and day. When the ship lay becalmed they waited for her.

It was from the barque's deck Willie first lost sight of the North Star and saw, opening up to the south, the splendid constellation of the Southern Cross and the Centaurs, and saw for the first time the sun setting astern to the north.

The crew of the barque brought in the New Year of 1872 in cold, sleety weather although it was summer. The return journey was much more eventful. Off the Cape of Good Hope she came close to losing some of her crew. The wind blew up and she heaved and tossed. For two days she rode under bare poles.

'Where the outward journey had been quick,' writes Willie, 'the return was dreich and weary. Large barnacles and great masses of seaweed slowed progress. For two weeks we lay becalmed off the Azores.'

Harsher times lay ahead for Willie. In September 1872, he joined a three-masted windjammer, the *Anne Mary*, at

Glasgow. She had been built at Newport, Monmouth, in 1850, and was registered at Liverpool. She was 789 tons and was to become his home for twenty months, as he explains:

> The *Anne Mary* was an old ship. In her early days she had been an East India frigate ship, and the ring bolts were still in her decks to which they used to lash down the guns. She was strong. You could have run her on to a reef and she would have held together.
>
> But the masts were soft wood and rotten. They had been too often to the southward to be much good. But they were good enough for a lot of old salts to adventure on. The yards were not much better and when it came to lying out on them in the roaring forties or off the pitch of the Horn, it was touch and go whether you came in again. The crew would swear on these yards. You never heard the like.

Willie caught a crew member by the jacket, after he had let go the jackstay and been a foot on his way to Davy Jones's locker, and jerked him on again to the bellying topsail.

'He swore like a trooper to relieve his feelings.'

An ancient mariner at the docks in Glasgow who knew the *Anne Mary* from her early days tried to put Robertson off boarding.

'Her pump haun'les are too bricht,' said the old-timer.

'I took it for granted he was a croaker,' said Willie, 'and did not permit his observations to influence me in any way.'

The *Anne Mary* was bound for Callao, chief seaport of Peru. She carried a cargo of coal, rice and machinery for a sugar plantation. On deck were three Skye terriers, a greyhound and a retriever bitch. These were passengers.

For three days and nights she lay off the Tail of the Bank at Greenock while attempts were made to muster a crew. When she put out Willie's first job was to take a spell at the pumps.

'In my ignorance I thought it was the correct thing for a wooden ship to leak a little. I was not even scared when the sailors came on board and said they were "in for it".'

The ship was not long at sea when Willie began to find out about the *Anne Mary*. 'When we had sailed across the Bay and down outside the northern tropics I discovered her timbers were alive with bugs.'

The problem was so acute the crew could not sleep in their bunks in hot weather. Willie bedded down on the deck wherever he could find room. When the vessel took on a cargo of cedar logs some months later the bugs were never seen afterwards.

Rats were another hazard they had to cope with. The ship was alive with them. They fed on the rice and when they came on deck to look for water the terriers went for them. The retriever never took to ratting, but the greyhound collared on to it and became expert.

'They ate my books and clothes and attacked us as we lay in bed. A pair of boots was a necessary adjunct to a sound sleep.'

Willie's first experience of the rats left him mortified:

I was awakened out of my sleep by something running about on top of me. I kicked out and was left alone for a little while. Back they came, four or five of them. I could see them in the light of the slush lamp. One night they attacked my feet. Sailors in fine weather have their feet bare and the skin thickens on the heels. It was this thick skin they were eating. It made me creep all over to find what they were about.

Willie bought a mongoose for half-a-sovereign from a cabin boy and trained it as a pet. He would not allow his fellow crewmen to feed it. The mongoose became an expert rat-catcher, justifying Willie's motive in buying it, and giving him peace at night. He took it into his bunk and it killed seven rats on the first night. It then killed eight, and on the third night six.

'Down by the Falkland Islands we ran into a deep gulf for fresh food and had a feast of fresh mutton. That night with an abundance of food on board the forecastle was black with rats.'

Two Swedish members of the crew fixed up a hatch on a belaying pin and strewed lumps of skin below it. This was an effective method of extermination. By pulling out the pin and letting the hatch drop they could kill over a score at a time.

The further the *Anne Mary* sailed the worse the problem of the leak became. Spells at the pump handles morning and night developed into half-hour spells every four hours. No sooner had seven bells struck on every watch than the pumps were manned.

'As we gave them three successive spells to allow for

gradual drawing of the water to the well, it was generally on the stroke of eight bells ere we finished.'

Down in the Southern Ocean the *Anne Mary* faced the sea at its cruellest.

> For nine months of the year the wind is from the westward and all the while the great seas rock and roll and chase one another across the vast unbroken stretch of ocean. The weather was cold, the months were September and October, spring time in these parts, and for more than six weeks we battled with the head wind and the raging billows. The ship creaked and groaned like a human being. Some of her timbers seemed to work backwards and forwards and wherever it came from the water kept steadily coming in. Six hours out of every four and twenty were spent at the pumps. Imagine what a half-hour spell at the pump handle means off Cape Horn.

The crew were subjected to pitiless snow and hail squalls. Waves thirty feet from trough to crest pitched the ship around like a leaf in a gale. They had to endure cold days and colder nights. Great seas discharged over one rail then over the other, sometimes rushing over the bows and falling from the fo'c'sle head on to the main deck with the force of a cataract.

The *Anne Mary* rolled and dived, making it impossible for the crew to stay on their feet without something to hold on by. Willie Robertson hung on for dear life to the pump handles, wet to the skin and unable to get any shelter. His feet and hands were numb. The horizon was foreshortened by day. The nights were black, relieved only by the white crests of the towering breakers.

After a six-week struggle they succeeded in getting the *Anne Mary* round the Horn and into the Pacific Ocean. As they sailed north the sea became smoother, the sun hotter, but the leakage grew worse. It got so bad when they reached Callao, that four of the hands, of whom Willie was one, were detailed to keep the ship clear of water by night. As they lay in the shelter of the rocks of San Lorenzo, off Callao, the crew realised there must be a hole in the ship. They put her in dry dock and found what they took to be the problem, a hole an inch and a half in diameter. It was sealed and the ship's bottom was given an overhaul. When they put to sea again the ship was dry as a bone. The crew thought they had seen the last of the pump handles and stored them below.

In addition to his mongoose Willie had a dog as a pet. He went ashore at Callao one day with other crew members and the dog. The men rowed back to the ship and the dog swam behind them. On board the dog began to writhe in agony and Willie found it was covered in parasites he could not pull off. The dog's suffering was not ended until one of the crew hit on the idea of allowing hens which were kept on board to pick the dog's coat clean. They devoured the parasites, which they regarded as a delicacy.

Antonio was a third pet which Willie had on board. He was a large, gaunt, orange-and-tawny-coloured cat whose scarred body and nicked ears told of many a savage battle. Willie had found Antonio half-starved and trapped in a dock enclosure. He answered the cat's pathetic mewing cries and rescued him taking him on board.

Antonio took to life at sea falling in with the task of keeping down the ships unwanted rodents. But Antonio missed the tide when the *Anne Mary* left one port of call in South America and was stranded ashore. The crew alerted a sister ship to pick Antonio up. He was rescued and brought back to Liverpool where he refused to quit his new-found home and ended his days aboard it.

From Callao the *Anne Mary* headed for Certino in Central America, then sailed to the Gulf of Funseco. At both her ports of call she shipped cedar. After spending the best part of six months in what Robertson thought the hottest part of the world the ship sailed for the Southern Ocean and home. The passage lasted over six months and Willie Robertson found it the most trying experience of his life.

'It effectively cured me of the sea,' said Willie, 'for though I spent two more years before the mast I never forgot the miseries.'

They still had the problem of rats, and then scurvy broke out. No sooner had they left the Gulf of Funseco than the *Anne Mary* once again took in water. The pump handles were replaced and the crew began what seemed an eternal spell of pumping. The watches constantly relieved one another and from then until they reached Gravesend the work on board was confined to setting and taking in sail, and pumping.

We were just able to keep the water down and no more. Many a time when we were in the tropics and coasting along South American land, we prayed that our efforts might be unsuccessful and that we might be compelled to take to the boats and make for land. But there was no such luck in store for us. Night and day we were at the handles. Between the spells we sat on the main hatch and fell asleep. We became regular pumping machines and there was not a man on board from the captain down who could keep at it for two hours at a stretch. As the scurvy became worse the officers had to help. Ropes were tied to the pump handles and the regular see-saw went on incessantly. By this time there was hardly a pair of boots on board the ship and in the coldest of nights on the verge of the Antarctic Circle the water discharged itself on bare feet which parted with the sense of feeling. It was a glad day, I can tell you, when we saw the white cliffs of England, and a still happier one when we turned our backs on the *Anne Mary* as she lay in the basin of the West India Docks.

The *Anne Mary* mysteriously went on fire in the Thames on her way to docking. The rats deserted her by the hundreds and she burned down to the deck. When the crew went ashore in London it was to find that the owner of the vessel had died.

'I wish you could have heard what the crew had to say about his post-mortem experience. If there is any truth in it the man who sends a leaky, rat-ridden, scurvy-promoting ship to sea is not to be envied.'

13

HOGMANAY INCIDENT

Mores, manners and morality have changed considerably since those days of the early 1950s and the Hogmanay Incident. It involved two young male police recruits – Willie and Andy.

Today it would be virtually unthinkable for two fully grown men to share a double bed. Back then it was perfectly acceptable and respectable to do so. Willie and Andy had a room let to them by Mrs McKell who had been looking after and feeding police recruits in her home for years.

Willie, come Hogmanay, had been encouraged at the end of his shift to celebrate the finish of the year and the looming of a new one. One drink became two and two became four. Things reached the stage where Willie, still in uniform, had to be taken home to Mrs McKell's house.

He went upstairs peaceably enough, but once there he insisted he was a bird and could fly. He opened the bedroom window to demonstrate his flying prowess and had one leg over the window sill before his colleagues intervened, saving him from serious injury.

The drink Willie had taken proved too much and he collapsed. This allowed his colleagues to undress him, lock the window and put him to bed. Willie was due back on duty on New Year's Day but could not be roused. This doleful news was conveyed to Sergeant John who was in the office less than a mile away.

'I'll rouse him,' said the sergeant, placing his uniform cap on his bald and highly knowledgeable head. He marched down to Mrs McKell's house. Mrs McKell burst into tears when she saw Sergeant John at her front door.

'Oh! Sergeant,' she cried. 'We cannae get him up.'

'I'll get him up,' said Sergeant John, expressing a confidence in his own ability which he felt was lacking in those around him. He strode upstairs to the bedroom Mrs McKell had let out to the two young policemen. Willie's roommate, Andy, had just come off duty and had climbed over Willie's recumbent body to the inside of the bed, against the wall, to get some much needed sleep.

This situation in no way deterred Sergeant John. When Willie failed to respond to the sound of the sergeant's voice, the sergeant removed his uniform cap, pushed up the sleeves of his jacket and began, with both hands, bouncing Willie up and down on the well-sprung bed. There was no response from Willie. He lay there, inert, comatose, unconscious. Refusing to be beaten, Sergeant John became more and more frantic in his efforts. Each time he gave Willie a vigorous thrust downwards Andy, on the other side of the bed against the wall, shot upwards in equally vigorous fashion in living proof, at least in Andy's case, of the validity of

Newton's third law of motion – for every force there is an equal and opposite force or reaction.

Andy, who was pretending to be fast asleep, could keep up the pretence no longer. His language was choice as he bounced up and down while Willie bounced down and up. Forming part of the backdrop to the scene stood Mrs McKell producing wells of tears as she saw her normally well-run establishment reduced to the level of a stage farce.

Realising he too had been beaten by Willie's alcohol intake, Sergeant John straightened his sleeves, donned his cap once more, and, without a word, marched out of the house, leaving behind a tearful landlady, a comatose constable and Andy, still trying to get some sleep.

The sergeant knew his inspector was due shortly, checking up on his men, and the sergeant liked to give the impression that he was running a tight, well-trimmed ship. He stood by Willie, covering for him, but later tore a strip off him in private. Later still he gave Willie a glowing reference which helped him gain promotion.

Andy, too, stood by Willie – in church as best man at his wedding.

14

BILL AITKEN

Penning a word portrait of an ebullient type like Bill Aitken is like trying to paint running water. You don't know where to start.

Bill's father, 'Lally' Aitken, was a tailor by occupation, but itchy feet took him to America in the bootlegging days. He left there hurriedly under instruction not to come back, and returned to Scotland. Lally became a lorry driver, but lost his licence. He took up work in an auction room handling second-hand furniture. He was handyman and dogsbody.

Lally's natural enterprise carried him down unexplored avenues. He bought up the stock of a funeral undertaker who was shutting down his business. With his drinking partner, Danny, he piled coffins heavens high on a barrow, wheeled them across town to an old shed and began making ironing boards for housewives who used them unaware of the original purpose for which the wood had been cut.

Lally found another use for the coffins. Curious schoolboys discovered it when they investigated raucous singing from the shed one afternoon. They found Danny and Lally each lying back in a coffin, clutching a near-empty whisky bottle.

Lally's business acumen died with the shock treatment he received to curb his drinking tendencies. Shock treatment was essential, when breakfast had become a raw egg washed down with methylated spirit.

Tel père, tel fils. Bill became unconventional in his behaviour. He joined the Fleet Air Arm, served as an air gunner, was twice torpedoed at sea and twice rescued. A wartime colleague advised Bill to try journalism and he did so, ending up as the editor of his local paper.

Readers who knew Bill affectionately dubbed him 'Stop Press' and he adopted this as a pseudonym under witty doggerel he wrote, which was good enough to prompt replies in kind – a sure indication of its effectiveness.

Bill had a tale to tell on every subject you cared to raise with him, and a story about everyone he knew. Though the reason for doing so has long since escaped my powers of recall, I once raised in his presence the name of Mr Gavin Clelland.

Mr Clelland was a surgical specialist with the Royal Army Medical Corps, serving with considerable distinction in Italy. He became a consultant surgeon and died in his hospital, reputedly from overwork, at the age of 46.

When I mentioned Gavin Clelland's name Bill Aitken immediately produced a story:

'He did my operation for piles,' said Bill. 'I remember we discussed it all beforehand. "What shape would you like?" he asked me. "I can give you spades, hearts, diamonds or clubs. But remember:

There's a divinity that shapes our ends,
Rough-hew them how we will.

15

GETTING A START

Bob Brown was lastingly grateful to George Goodfellow for taking him on to the editorial staff while fully aware that Bob would be called up for military service in a few weeks. It gave Bob the right, as the law stood, to come back to journalism if, and when, he returned from the war.

Bob survived and on his return quickly rose to national level, with the London *Times*. He mixed with homburg-hatted Hannen Swaffer, the Pope of Fleet Street, and Ian MacKay.

Ian was dux of Wick Academy in 1916 and made his way to London. He had a photographic memory, which reduced his need for shorthand. He always wrote with a fountain pen filled with bright blue ink. Ian famously wrote his own obituary:

> *When the time comes when I am not*
> *Some friend will mutter 'How his head was hot.'*
> *And some fair charmer when the tale is told*
> *Will sigh and murmur 'But his feet were cold.'*
> *But then I hope they'll walk off arm in arm*
> *And say together 'But his heart was warm.'*

Ian died suddenly on Blackpool esplanade after attending and reporting the Labour Party conference. At conference end he was always chosen to reply to the vote of thanks to the press. That was the year when Aneurin Bevan, angered by the coverage the Labour Party had been receiving, described the British press as the most prostituted in the world.

In his reply Ian excused himself for lapsing into Anglo-Saxon, but remarked how grateful he and his colleagues were, having been called bastards during the week, to be given a certificate of legitimacy at the end of it.

After his cremation in London Ian's colleagues took his ashes to the pub for a drink, then accidentally spilled them in the gutter and saw them washed down the drain.

'Oh, well,' remarked one. 'It's how he would have wanted to go.'

Bob Brown recalled seeing Ian seated at a table at the end of a conference session, trying to begin the piece he wanted to telephone to his paper, the *News Chronicle*. Ian scribbled on the sheet before crunching it up into a ball and throwing it on the floor in disgust. He took another sheet and repeated this. The floor was soon littered with discarded, crumpled sheets of paper.

Finally, said Bob, he took a fresh sheet and wrote at the top 'Brighton – Thursday,' and gasped in relief: 'At last I've got something bloody right!'

16

GOING THE DISTANCE

For a nineteenth century Church of Scotland minister Reverend Roderick Lawson was far travelled, getting to the Holy Land. But Roderick was considerably outdistanced by several of his former fellow pupils at school.

Peter Sinclair had little military spirit about him. Yet after emigrating to America with a view to bettering himself, Peter was among the first 75,000 to step forward when the US Government called for volunteers to oppose the Confederates in the Civil War and Peter died, shot in the breast, at Bull Run on Manassas Plains in Virginia.

'Shot in the breast – I like that,' said Roderick. 'It is an honourable certificate of character.'

Joseph Coulter survived the Crimean War, though how he did so reads like an extended chapter from *The Pilgrim's Progress*. At Sebastopol he got a musket ball through his right arm and one in the left breast which also went through him.

'The wound is three or four inches higher in front than it is in the rear, because they were higher than we were,' Joseph wrote to his parents from Scutari Barracks, Constantinople, on 25 October 1864.

In the battle Joseph was struck on the right arm by a piece of shrapnel. After that he got a musket ball through his left thigh. Another broke the middle finger of his right hand. The quartermaster sergeant happened to pass by.

'Hillo,' says he. 'My dear fellow, where are you struck?'

I said, 'Well, sir, I am struck with four balls and a bit of a shell.'

'Good God and are you not dead yet? I must get you carried to the hospital.'

The quartermaster sergeant was as good as his word and got Joseph moved to Scutari Hospital where Florence Nightingale was in charge. Joseph later had a shilling-a-day pension and British, Turkish and French medals to show for his exploits.

Two of Roderick's old schoolmates ran stores at the Australian gold diggings. Another commanded a steamer on the Ohio River. One became a minister in New Zealand, one a teacher in Australia, and another a chief engineer on a Cunard ship. Two drank themselves to death and one committed suicide.

One chum of particular interest was the lad who used to read *Caesar* with Roderick at school. He emigrated to New Zealand and married the daughter of a Maori chief. She was a well-educated girl and could play piano. But the bridegroom's father back home was not too certain of New Zealand life. 'By Jove,' he said, 'she'll eat him some morning.'

17

ANDY, JIMMY, DAVE, JOHN AND DAME MARGOT

I never saw Andy Murdoch wear anything other than his bow-tied, maître d'hôtel garb, no matter the hour on the clock. Any gathering at Prestwick Airport seemed incomplete without Andy. He was the airport butler. At press conferences he had the alarming habit of pouring newsmen triples which we never refused, irrespective of the time of day or the transport in use.

Andy's florid features told clearly that he held the key to the cabinet and was a frequent visitor there on his own behalf. One day he collapsed and died without warning. One of his many friends summoned a doctor. The GP who arrived did not know Andy and had never seen him.

The friend explained: 'Doctor, Andy has worked here for years and has never had a day's illness in his life.'

'Well,' said the doctor, a bit dismissively, 'you can say that his first illness was his last one.'

Jimmy Jeffs was commandant at Prestwick Airport for years. He was a tall, impressive individual who got things done by his mere presence and a few words. When Jimmy left Prestwick he moved to London Heathrow where his duties included meeting the Queen as she stepped off a plane from abroad. His self-provided curriculum vitae indicated that he had been a member of air crews flying her father, George VI, during the Second World War.

Jimmy had his own chauffeur at the airport. A near neighbour of mine, Dave Frew, took on the job when the predecessor retired. Dave went to see his new boss. Jimmy handed him the car keys.

'Your first duty, Frew,' said Jimmy, 'will be to go down to my car and take ten thousand miles off the clock. I'm selling it this afternoon.'

Dave Frew had been chauffeur for years to John C. Sword who engineered the amalgamation of several small independent bus companies in Ayrshire of the 1920s. He created a viable service for those days when few people owned a motor car. Scurrilous gossip put it about that John paid Ayr's town clerk a backhander to shut down the town's 30-year-old corporation tram service to drive passengers on to his buses.

John was an avid collector. In his home, Craigweil, on Ayr's seafront, he had a remarkable collection of clocks, some of them exotic timepieces. Dave told me that John learned about an old shepherd who owned a clock which interested John.

'I drove him to see this chap and the two of them argued over it. But the shepherd was more stubborn than John and refused to sell it, even after John, exasperated, threw his chequebook on the table and invited him to write his own price on it.'

Steam-driven model-railway engines formed part of John's wonderful empire of transport. He also owned a piece of Russell Flint artwork which attracted some attention. But John's best-known collection was his unique gathering of veteran and vintage motor cars which he stored on an Ayrshire farm. Many items were auctioned off after John's death. I remember going to see the cars on show for the sale and meeting Jimmy Logan, the theatre and television entertainer, who was looking for a suitable item to buy. I don't think he got one.

In transport terms John C. Sword was a far-seeing person. He paid a yearly fee to a farmer for the right to use one of his fields as a runway. It later became part of Prestwick Airport. The demands of war ensured that Prestwick Airport expanded rapidly. When the Japanese attack on Pearl Harbour led to the United States of America entering the war, the US Army Air Force took over and expanded much of the airport and remained there for many years, long after it had reverted to a civilian role, largely for transatlantic journeys.

The airport found itself taking on another task – that of a bolthole for other British airports when they were hampered by fog. Prestwick's fog-free reputation brought to the terminal Dame Margot Fonteyn when her flight was diverted from London.

This sent newsmen scurrying to interview her. Dame Margot was up to her elegant earlobes in the mystery of her disappearing husband. He was a diplomat involved in a coup d'état in Panama. She was involved with him and the two were charged with attempted gun-smuggling from their yacht off the coast of Panama. She was deported.

Dame Margot appeared in the interview room wearing the most sumptuous clothing and smiling serenely.

'Dame Margot,' I asked her 'have you any idea where your husband is?'

Dame Margot proved to be every bit as wily a diplomat as her husband, Roberto Arias: 'Oh,' she said. 'I was hoping you would be able to tell me.'

18

À LA RECHERCHE DU CONTE PERDU

Every good story is at risk of plagiarism. This makes tracking the good tale to its source a diverting piece of detective work. It can take us back to Rome and the days of Cicero, or Athens and the golden age of Pericles. And beyond.

Mine took me no farther than the musty halls of the High Court in London before the start of the First World War.

The dreary proceedings and the wearisome work of handling Irish land claims went on day after tedious day. A prominent figure on the scene was Sergeant Sullivan who found himself, on a warm afternoon in a stuffy courtroom, facing a tetchy judge who got tetchier and tetchier as the case dragged on.

Alexander Sullivan would later take on the job of defending, unsuccessfully, Sir Roger Casement on a treason charge when all others at the bar refused to touch it. But that was later. This was now.

Sullivan's paperwork took him into more and more tiny detail which threatened to be unending. His lordship became completely exasperated.

'Mr Sullivan,' he exploded, 'do your clients not realise the law is not capable of dealing with such trifles? Have they never heard *De minimis non curat lex*?'

Sullivan adopted the blandest imaginable smile, clutched the lapels of his jacket and drew himself up to his full height:

'My lord' he told the bench, 'in the bogs of Connemara they speak of little else.'

19

ANGELA'S GHOST

Alan Dent never lost his Scots accent despite spending much of his life, from the age of 21, in London. His father, John, was an avid reader of Thomas Hardy's novels and named Alan's sister Tess. Alan, at the end of his university studies, went on a walking tour of Wessex. From there he travelled to London, knocked on the door of drama critic James Agate and became his secretary.

Alan, already a serious student of Shakespeare, learned the trade of dramatic criticism so well that he became theatre critic on the *Manchester Guardian* and, later, the *News Chronicle*. This brought him back to Scotland every year for the Edinburgh Festival.

I remember accompanying him on a visit to Culzean Castle and Country Park. As we walked into the castle I was whistling, for some reason, the Schubert song 'To Music'.

'That was one of my choices,' said Alan, 'on *Desert Island Discs*.'

Alan had been Roy Plomley's guest on the popular radio programme in early 1944 when the war against

Germany was nearing the invasion of Normandy beaches.

'The BBC would not allow it to be sung in German,' said Alan, who could not appreciate why it was necessary to carry censorship so far. Schubert had been a long time dead, but his music, for Alan, lived on.

Earlier, on a June morning in 1941, Alan was walking along The Strand. People on the streets of London were shovelling up glass from windows shattered by heavy bombing the previous night in the Blitz. Ahead of him Alan saw an elderly lady, dressed in Victorian or Edwardian clothing.

Not wanting to appear too forward he overtook the figure, intending to glance in a shop window before looking back for a full-face view. But she had disappeared.

Alan realised the only place she could have gone into was Coutts Bank in The Strand. He hurried there to speak to the commissionaire who had just unlocked the door for the bank's normal 10 a.m. opening.

'Good morning. Has a lady dressed in black come in?' he asked.

'How could she, sir,' said the doorkeeper. 'I have just this second opened the door.'

The incident left Alan mystified. But he could not leave it there. He launched an investigation which led him to conclude he had seen the ghost of Angela Burdett-Coutts.

Angela, I suspect, was the anonymous donor who put up the money which gave Edinburgh its statue of Greyfriars Bobby. She was generous in nineteenth-century charitable work but found herself pestered by beggars at every level. She was long the power behind Coutts Bank, which handled finances for royalty and much of Britain's aristocracy. It was wealth which did not come directly to her.

Angela's great-grandfather served as Lord Provost of Edinburgh. Her grandfather married his brother's maid-servant and had three daughters, all of whom married well. The youngest, Sophia, wed Sir Francis Burdett, Angela's father.

The grandfather, Thomas Coutts, gained control of the already established bank and became the richest man in London. But the bank and its money did not pass directly to any of his daughters. They had all been well provided for, when Angela's mother died, following years of a mental breakdown. Thomas married, a fortnight later, the actress, Harriot Mellon, with whom he had been on intimate terms for years. He was over 70 years of age on his remarriage. Harriot was thirty years younger.

This second marriage caused great friction in the family. It took place in 1815, the year after Angela was born. Thomas lived on till 1822. On his death he left all the Coutts wealth to Harriot. She remained a widow for five years, but then remarried. Her second husband, who had proposed three times, was William Aubrey de Vere, ninth Duke of St Albans, who was twenty-five years her junior.

This made Harriot a duchess. She wrote to Sir Walter Scott, hoping he would write her life story and sending him an inkwell for the job. Harriot outlived her second husband and, when she died childless in 1837, she left the entire Coutts fortune to her first husband's granddaughter, Angela.

Charles Dickens was among the advisors Angela had, and he suggested ways of using her wealth on charitable work. He dedicated one of his books, *Martin Chuzzlewit*, to her.

When the import of French lace caused the destruction of handloom weaving in parts of Scotland, Angela underwrote the emigration costs of many weavers to Australasia.

Angela had been on good terms with the Duke of Wellington, and sought to marry him in early 1847 when she was 33 and he was nearly 78 and old enough to be her grandfather. The Duke wrote to her, advising her not to throw herself away on a man so much her senior. It was advice she took.

Angela was also linked in common gossip with Louis Napoleon, nephew of the man the Duke had defeated at the Battle of Waterloo in 1815. But he married Spanish princess Eugenie de Montijo and she became Empress of the Second Empire, which Louis created in France after its last king, Louis Philippe, was dethroned in a coup d'état.

Angela helped Sir Henry Irving, funding some of his productions. When he died in October 1905, Angela, in her nineties, allowed her splendid house in Piccadilly to be used to let his many admirers view his body, lying in state in her dining room, before his cremation and Westminster Abbey funeral.

Angela's Piccadilly home had been a favourite spot for Queen Victoria, then a good friend, to sit and watch the traffic. It was here, Victoria said, she could do this without it stopping because of her. But all that ended abruptly when Angela married, at the age of 67, her American secretary, William Ashmead-Bartlett, who was forty years her junior. This provoked much public ribaldry and many jokes. Victoria called her a silly old woman and stopped inviting her to anything but formal occasions at Buckingham Palace.

This in no way upset Angela. She lived on to the age of 92, outliving Victoria, and died on 30 December 1906.

Little of this was known to Alan Dent when he began looking in to Angela's story. Alan, like the investigative journalist he was, soon made it his business.

Before he moved out of London to live in Beaconsfield, along the street where G. K. Chesterton had his home, Alan, whenever he was in the area, would walk the length of The Strand, hoping to see once again the apparition he was convinced had been the ghost of Angela Burdett-Coutts. He never did.

20

WILLIE CARROCHER

Willie changed the spelling of his name from Carragher to remove what he thought was Irish in it and give it a more Scots appearance. He was a Gaelic enthusiast and learned the language, self-taught from textbooks.

He fronted BBC cameras for the Mod. But before that he worked for the Scottish Office in Edinburgh, going on to join the Commonwealth Office, doing preparatory work for royal visits abroad. Prior to all this Willie worked on the staff of James Shaw Grant's newspaper, *The Stornoway Gazette*, and was able to appreciate life in the Outer Hebrides. Work there included court reporting.

Willie found a particular case intriguing. It involved alleged poaching. Two deer had been rifle-shot and the suspicions of the police centred on an elderly crofter in the village of Achmore, eight miles from Stornoway. They made investigation and eventually brought a charge against the suspect crofter.

The matter came to court and Willie sat through the trial after the accused had pled not guilty.

So reluctant and protective were neighbour-witnesses

who had been cited that they were totally disinclined to provide any evidence which would corroborate what the police said. The presiding sheriff found himself unable to return anything other than a not-proven verdict.

Willie chose not to report the case in the newspaper. But an issue of the *Gazette* shortly afterwards carried an anonymous limerick in an appropriate column:

There was an old man of Achmore
Who had rifle and bullets in store
And strange was it not
That two deer got shot
And himself neffer out of the door.